Journey to the promised land

Story by Penny Frank
Illustrated by Tony Morris

THE LION
STORY BIBLE

11

TRING · BATAVIA · SYDNEY

The Bible tells us
how God chose the Israelites to be his
special people. He made them a
promise that he would always love
and care for them. But they must
obey him.

This is the story of how God led
them to the new land of Canaan. You
can find it in your own Bible, in
Exodus, Numbers and Joshua.

Copyright © 1986 Lion Publishing

Published by
Lion Publishing plc
Icknield Way, Tring, Herts, England
ISBN 0 85648 736 8
Lion Publishing Corporation
1705 Hubbard Avenue, Batavia,
Illinois 60510, USA
ISBN 0 85648 736 8
Albatross Books Pty Ltd
PO Box 320, Sutherland, NSW 2232, Australia
ISBN 0 86760 520 0

First edition 1986
Reprinted 1987

Printed and bound in Hong Kong

**British Library Cataloguing in
Publication Data**

Frank, Penny
Journey to the promised land. – (The
Lion Story Bible; v. 11)
1. Exodus, The – Juvenile
literature 2. Bible stories,
English – O.T. Exodus
I. Title   II. Morris, Tony,
1938 Aug 2 –
222'.1209505   BS1245.5

ISBN 0-85648-736-8

**Library of Congress
Cataloging-in-Publication Data**

Frank, Penny.
Journey to the promised land.
(The Lion Story Bible; 11)
1. Exodus, The—Juvenile literature.
2. Jews—History—To 1200 B.C.—
Juvenile literature. [1. Exodus, The.
2. Jews—History—To 1200 B.C.
3. Bible stories—O.T.] I. Morris, Tony,
ill. II. Title. III. Series: Frank, Penny.
Lion Story Bible; 11.
BS680.E9F72 1986   222'.109505
85-24091
ISBN 0-85648-736-8

The Israelites had lived in the land of Egypt for a long time. They had often wanted to live in a land of their own. But they were slaves and the king would not let them go.

God gave them a leader called Moses and he made the king say, 'Yes, you can go.' So Moses led the Israelites out of Egypt.

But the king of Egypt changed his mind. Suddenly the Israelites heard the sound of horses behind them. The Egyptians were chasing after them! They didn't know where to run.

There was a wide river in front of them. They looked at Moses in dismay.

'Don't be afraid,' Moses said. 'Watch and see what God will do.'

Then Moses held his stick out over the water. All night long a strong wind blew. It made a dry pathway through the river. The Israelites hurried across.

But when the Egyptians tried to follow, the water came back. and they could not cross. The Israelites were safe. They danced and sang for joy.

But before long God's people began to grumble. What was there to eat and drink in the desert?

'Trust me,' God said. And every morning he sent them special food. It lay on the ground like frost. It tasted like biscuits made with honey. The people called it manna.

When they cried out for meat, God sent some birds called quails to eat.

When they complained that they were thirsty, God told Moses to strike a big rock with his stick. And water poured out for them to drink.

God took great care of his people in the desert.

Then God said to Moses, 'I need to talk
to you about the way I want my people
to live.'

The people were camped at the foot of
Mount Sinai. So Moses went up the
mountain to talk to God.

God gave Moses the laws he wanted
the Israelites to keep. They are called the
ten commandments.

8

Moses was gone so long that the Israelites grew tired of waiting.

'What's the good of a God you can't see?' they said. So they melted down the gold from their jewelry and made it into a model of a calf.

'Let's pretend that this is God,' they said. They danced around the calf.

When Moses came back he was very angry. He smashed the calf into tiny pieces.

The people were very sorry for what they had done. They promised from now on to keep God's laws.

God had told Moses to make him a
special tent. God's tent would be set up
in the middle of the camp for everyone
to see. Inside, it was very beautiful.

It had a special room where a copy of God's laws was kept. The laws were stored inside a box covered in gold, and creatures made of gold covered the lid with their wings.

Everywhere the Israelites went, they would take God's tent and the special box with them, to remind them of God.

One day, as they journeyed, God said to Moses, 'Across that river is Canaan, the land I am giving to you. Send some men over to look. Then they can tell you what it is like.'

So Moses sent twelve men to look at the land. They brought back bunches of grapes.

'It is a good land,' they said. 'But we can't go in — there are giants to fight.'

But Joshua and Caleb, two of the men, said, 'There's no need to be afraid if God is with us.'

The Israelites would not listen to Joshua and Caleb.

'We're not going to fight giants,' they said. 'Let's choose a new leader and go back to Egypt.'

'When will you learn to trust me?' God asked them. 'I have taken care of you all this time. I have kept all my promises. And still you won't trust me! Now you will spend forty years more in the desert.'

Nothing would stop the people grumbling. Then one day there were snakes all around the tents. Many of the people were bitten by the snakes and died.

'It's because we didn't obey God,' the people said, and they begged God to forgive them.

God told Moses to put a metal snake onto a tall pole.

'God says that you must trust him,' Moses told them. 'If you have been bitten, look up at the metal snake and God will heal you.'

So the people obeyed God and they were healed.

The Israelites had not trusted God to take them into the new land. Now Moses was too old to be their leader.

God told Moses that Joshua was to be the new leader.

So Moses took Joshua out in front of all the Israelites.

'This is the man God has chosen to take you into your new land,' he told them.

The people were very sad when Moses died. He had been their leader for a long time.

Now that they had learned to trust God
they were ready to follow Joshua into
the new land of Canaan — the land
promised to them by God.

The Lion Story Bible is made up of 52 individual stories for young readers, building up an understanding of the Bible as one story — God's story — a story for all time and all people.

The Old Testament section (numbers 1–30) tells the story of a great nation — God's chosen people, the Israelites — and God's love and care for them through good times and bad. The stories are about people who knew and trusted God. From this nation came one special person, Jesus Christ, sent by God to save all people everywhere.

The adventures of God's people on their way to the promised land are scattered through the books of Exodus and Numbers. The ten commandments come in Exodus, chapter 20; the golden calf in Exodus 32; the special tent in Exodus 25 and 26. The story of the spies is from Numbers, chapter 13.

Even though God had rescued them from slavery in Egypt, his people still found it hard to trust him. And how they grumbled — despite the fact that he gave them all they really needed. The long journey taught them many lessons, and they began to learn to do as God said.

The next story in the series, number 12: *The battle of Jericho*, tells how God took his people into their new land and gave them their first great victory.